A biography of the luckiest, most unlucky guy

# MELANOMA

## Then why am I still here!

I am a prize fighter, although no one has heard of me. I am up there with the real prize fighters, such as George Foreman, Rocky Marciano, Mohamed Ali. I never won millions of dollars, lived in mansions, or drove fancy cars, but I stand with literally millions of people around the world, who are also prize fighters and no one knows our names. I won the fight of my life, with the best coaches, Jesus Christ, my wife Mary, M.D.Anderson Cancer Center in Houston, Texas and quite a few Doctors, North, South, East and West Texas, who have to offer their experience to help me win this battle! This is my story that began many years ago, and everything is True! Along with Humor, I used it to help me and others affected by Cancer, or know someone who has or had it, GOD is with you. Ask him for his Spiritual Healing. This is the Updated version of my book.

I'll begin with my arrival in 1955, Detroit, Michigan. Where the really cool cars were being built, and we didn't realize how cool, for about another Twenty years. My parents were married three months prior to my birth, and I didn't know this until I was Forty years old when my father passed away at Eighty Eight years young and just shy of his Eighty Ninth. My father was born in 1906, and mom in 1917, mom went to be with dad in 1998 three years after him. The name alone, "DALTON" in the 1800's brings back what the history books describe as, Good going Bad. It revolved around a family of lawmen that were wronged and decided to get revenge on banks & trains. Both of which they weren't too good at doing, and only one lived after being shot full of holes and spending time in prison. I doubt I'm related by blood, but I sure followed their luck. Mine started as a toddler. We lived at 9541 Stoepel St. Detroit, Michigan. Our telephone number was, TX4-1237. My first school was Ruth Ruff and a short block or two from home. Our home was a two family flat. We lived upstairs, and my fathers relatives, downstairs. I started off easy, and while I was dressed up, new shoes and ready to hit the town, mom and dad got dressed. When they were ready to leave for dinner, they found me standing in the toilet, new shoes and all. At a very young age I was headed downstairs with a plastic pair of sunglasses on. When I quit falling I was taken to the hospital, and three stitches were placed above my left eye. I don't remember this happening, but mom did and the scar can barely be seen in my eyebrow. I decided to taste coffee one morning, while mom was sitting at the kitchen table talking to a relative, I reached up and grabbed her cup of scalding hot coffee, before she could stop me. When my T-shirt was pulled off of me, the skin came with it. I now have Two scars and I just started! If you grew up with questions such as, Can I do that? Will it fit? Will it hurt? I tried them all. I stuck my head in the chair rail of one dining room chair that went to a fancy set. At that age I wasn't told of boy's/man's ears. A man's ears are just like a wall anchor you would stick into a sheetrock, to hold up a picture. The only difference is a man's ear doesn't need a screw to make it strong so it doesn't come out, his ears do that! Easy to go in and one rail needed to be broken to free my head. It scared me so bad, I did it again but this time I used the Banister on the stairs. The results were the same! I cannot remember my age, maybe Five or Six, I told my mother I had a headache. She went to the medicine cabinet and the baby aspirin bottle was empty. I remember the trip to the hospital and being told not to fall asleep. I also remember having my stomach pumped and the baby aspirins found. I was a little Toot growing up, and must have added years to my parents life. My mother was a Beautician and had customers come to the house once in a while. I must have seen this and went into her bedroom and poured a bottle of Liniment on my head. It flowed down into my eyes, and another hospital visit. I was too scared to open my eyes. It burned so bad and even though they were cleaned out, for two weeks I was blind and the doctor finally had to pry my eyes open, for me to believe It wouldn't hurt and I was ok.

Time passed before my next stunt and it was a doozie for a kid with my luck. There were several kids outside in our driveway playing so I climbed up on the driveway gate, got about waist high when a kid ran into it with his bicycle. It knocked me over the gate and I landed on top of my head. When I finally got up no one was there, every one of them ran away leaving me without even checking to see if I was hurt. I had to climb up three flights of stairs, to get to our back door and tell mom what had happened. This hospital visit was an overnight stay. I had a slight concussion and mom said I looked like a Racoon with my face being black and blue. I was so small growing up, my fathers nickname for me was, Pill. At school I was bullied, my lunch money was stolen by a kid threatening me. He began tapping me on the head with a pencil and it was happening just after the concussion. Mom found out and went into Mother Mode and the school heard every word she had to say! Our neighborhood was changing and the White folks were leaving, and Black folks moving in. I had no issues with the Black folks, or kids. It was the White kids who were bullying me. My friend, a black boy, came home with me from school for lunch and my aunt was waiting for us. She was taking care of me while my parents were away.

My friend and I decided to have some fun, and dad had a Bobcat mounted, which he had taken while hunting. I got the Bobcat out and hid it around the corner, while my friend picked up my cat. He tossed Spike around the corner, in front of the Bobcat. I made a wild growl, and Spike began to spit, scream, and Crapped all over everything he pointed his tail at, including my friend. I solved the old question; Can you have the Crap scared out of you, YES! My aunt had to clean up my friend, so we could go back to school and then clean the walls, carpet, furniture and all.

## My first move into a new neighborhood

I don't remember the move to Redford Township, a suburb of Detroit, but I do remember getting lost on the first day of school, while trying to find my way home. A new school of all White kids and trouble followed me. I was a small kid, not from the neighborhood, a Bully's Dream! They used me as a punching bag, to show off in front of the normal kids. Most of this happened at school, but there was a time at my home, a tall skinny kid followed by his friends showed up to do his showoff. I finally got tired of being used to slap around and one day a kid was doing just that, I hit him back! That day I began to grow up. I started to hang out with an older kid and both him and his brother didn't like bully's, but also weren't out looking for them. These two brothers were from a Catholic raised family, and were good folks. With me growing and my father buying me a 110 pound weight set, which I put together outdoors and then my brother showed up. He was 21 years older than me, same mother and different father. He was in the Korean war and a Paratrooper and came home, alive. When he saw the weights sitting there, with one hand he lifted that 110 pounds over his head! It took me several years before I could do the same. I learned how to work on bicycles and had fun doing it for friend's. I took a car steering wheel and placed it on a bicycle, cut two apart and made a bicycle built for two. This was done with broken pieces of bikes I found & all worked good. That friend showed me places we could ride to and watch kids' ball games, and chase balls that were floating in the river after storms came through. There was a Rough River Nature Center, we rode to and visited. This all was quite far from our homes, but our parents worked and didn't know about our rides and swimming in a river. After the swimming and collecting things floating by, we would pull Leeches off each other and head home. One day I was following some friends, all of us on our bikes and several blocks away from home. We walked through one of the guys' yard, hopped over the chain link fence and across the field behind his house. They had dug a hole and covered it with tree limbs and leaves. In a kid's view, it was awesome! Then someone yelled, here comes the owner and he's got a shotgun. I didn't look to see, I just ran for that fence to jump over. When I was about there I found a hole and down I went. The kids behind me were now on top of me and it seemed like a second, there was no one around but me. I tried to stand and my ankle hurt from adding weight on it. I had to hop to the fence, climb over it, hop through the yard and didn't know if I could ride my bike. I tried and had no pain while peddling, so off I went towards home. When I rode to the back door, I had to crawl into the house and let my parents know what had happened. Another hospital visit and a broken ankle. I received a cast and crutches, but never saw anybody with any gun and I was the one injured! I was stuck at home where nothing could happen to me. I remember when our neighbors moved to Florida and it wasn't too long afterwards, I saw their daughter in the neighborhood.

Her brother was at the beach with a friend and they dug a hole in a dune. While he was in it, the whole thing collapsed, smothering him to death. He was younger than I and now gone. It scared me, because my brother and his family in 1966, moved to Arlington, Texas. My first experience traveling by plane was a trip to Texas in a Propeller Plane. I was a bit scared but excited to see Texas. It was awesome, wide open places and beautiful country. Plus they talked funny! We moved to Arlington in 1967 and I started school.

## Texas move to a new life

This was the best move we have made, I think! Most of the kids were friendly to me, being in a new school, new state and city, I fit right in. I was practicing to be on the football team, but I just couldn't understand the plays I was supposed to memorize and I was interested in other things. I had two fights, right off the bat. My math class was in a temporary building, just outside of the main school. I took a seat and two black kids came in and sat at my table. The teacher was waiting for everyone to get to class and the big guy sitting with me, took a swing at me. The fight was on and for no reason. I knew the two guys, but never had trouble with them. The teacher left to get help and before she could enter the school, we motioned for her to return. The fight was over, no one was hurt, all it did was scare the teacher. I suppose it was a show of strength, because we never had issues again. I took a Scuba Diving course in Dallas and became a Certified (NASDS) National Association of Skin Diving Schools, based out of California. My open water certification was at Lake Grapevine, Grapevine, Texas. Several years later I took an Advanced course, and then a Rescue Divers course. I was working on my Dive Masters, something came up and I never finished it. A very good friend of mine was getting married and asked me to give her away. I was with the family when her father's heart stopped and then came back to life until she and her mom were holding him. He then passed away. I agreed to give his daughter, my friend, away at her wedding. On the evening before the wedding, I drove the bride's mom and the groom's dad to the church for the practice run. Afterwards we headed back to the mom's home, after all it was her car. We were sitting a block from the church at the stop sign, waiting to turn right. I looked up and saw a Ford F-150, headed straight for us. We were hit just behind the driver's side door and the car ended up in the yard of the Library after clearing the curb. All three of us were injured. We were hit by a Drunk Driver! All three of us spent the wedding in the hospital, which we insisted they continue with. My life was "normal" except for the time I was bitten in the eyelid by a Chinese Hooded Rat. It wasn't his fault, and the doctor had to call all of his people in to tell them what happened. The doctor advised I wouldn't die of Rabies and that made me feel better, until he said they can carry Bubonic Plague, but not Rabies. My mother thought he was funny, due to him wearing two different colored socks. A few years later I was driving a Semi cross country and got a late start out of the Dallas terminal, due to them losing the keys to the truck. I was headed to Miami, Florida, with a load of home insulation and wanted to make up for some time so I took a different route to Interstate 10. This would take me through Opelousas and Lafayette Louisiana to catch the Interstate. Just as I entered Opelousas, I heard a loud bang and thought I had a tire blow out. The truck was acting fine, and then a second bang took the windshield out of my truck. I was being shot at and I headed for the first exit to get off the highway. I pulled into a convenience store that was closing and he noticed how shook up I was and called the Sheriff's Department. They came out and looked at the truck, then said get in, let's go looking for someone. We found a Black man who lived in Opelousas, sitting in a gas station and his windshield was shot out. That was the first shot and it ripped across his windshield. The second shot, one that hit my truck, hit just above my head and looked like a Shotgun Slug shattering the windshield into my face and truck. The deputy advised me that it wasn't the first time it has happened and no one has been caught. My company advised me to go to hospital and get checked out and after getting a room at the motel, I did just that. My blood pressure was very high, I was covered in small pieces of glass with a few small bleeding areas from it. Otherwise, I was tired, and wanted a shower and sleep. A nurse at the hospital volunteered to take me back to the motel, after they were done, I accepted. On the way to her car, I fell off of the edge of the sloping ramp entering the hospital. The nurse advised me to have it x-rayed and I refused. I just wanted a good night's sleep! The next morning my ankle was so swollen, I couldn't put my boots on. I was on the next bus headed home, after setting up another truck to pick up the load, and someone else to drive the truck, after they fixed the windshield. My wife and I bought a nine acre lot in Hamilton county, outside of Hamilton, Texas and have been spending time there when we had it to do. It was a Two bedroom mobile home, with a large front covered porch, water was a deep well and tasted good. After I could walk I packed up and moved down to our country home. I got bored having fun and applied for a job at a convenience store, evening shift. I enjoyed it and the customers. A far cry from the hustle of a big city, or driving cross country. I was asked to take the manager's job and I accepted. In my spare time I took up Rattlesnake hunting, as a hobby and to help ranchers in the area that were having dogs and livestock bitten. I made my own cages and at first I didn't add handles. One night a storm was headed in, so I began to move the cages onto the porch. I picked one up just as the rattler struck at my hand and I let go fast. He got some skin, no blood and all the cages were updated with handles.

## A total life change

After my life fell apart, bad divorce, it was time to change occupations and I decided to become a Correctional Officer for Texas Department Of Criminal Justice. It took over a year and many phone calls to get a test for the job. After my approval and training, I was given the Dalhart Unit as my assigned unit, just outside Dalhart, Texas. I had no idea where that was, but I had about three days to be there and ready to work. The weekend before showing up at my assigned unit, I was in Port Aransas, Texas fishing in beautiful weather. The morning I walked out of the motel room in Dalhart, Texas, I was chipping ice off of my windshield so I could see. When my first pay came in, I ordered a Parka to wear to work, and it was a very good idea to do so. I was put in charge at a gate inside the main area of the compound, while a blizzard was hitting the area. I was warm and if the inmates wanted to eat, or go to certain areas, they had to pass by my post. This is the only time in Texas, I got stuck in the snow in my truck, twice. The most embarrassing part, it was in my driveway both times! The Correctional Officers job was Security, making sure the inmates don't escape, kill one another or us, riot, create gang activity within the walls of the prison, or through the mail, and so much more, Contraband, search inmates bunks and belongings, for weapons-homemade or not, drugs, money, notes/letters, to gang members, tobacco and more. There is so much more Officers must do, to keep peace in a locked up community. I started on the second shift and after learning the ways of the prison, I put in for day shift. I was there about five months when my mother fell in a nursing home and had to have surgery. I left Dalhart to come be with her in Mansfield, Texas. My brother had put her in the nursing home, to help her gain strength in her legs. After the surgery, she was brought back to the nursing home to recover. I finally had to head back to Dalhart prison and mom never knew I was there. I finally got home, called the unit and told them I was back, so I'd be there in the morning. My phone rang and my mother had aspirated and died shortly afterwards. After the funeral and collecting myself, I went into a work routine. A C.O. (correctional officer) and myself were assigned to transport inmates from Dalhart Unit, to a hospital in Amarillo, Texas. We had to stay at the hospital in Amarillo, until we were relieved by a second shift crew. The co that was with me was new to prison work and his wife was a nurse at the Dalhart hospital. He began to tell me about a lady at the hospital I needed to meet. I said ok and left it at that. I had just bought my Harley, it was still too cold to ride and I didn't need to meet a gal at the hospital! He wouldn't drop it, so I called her and we talked for a month or so on the phone. Then one day I had a Doctors appointment which his office was across from the hospital. I went into the hospital to see what she looked like and I couldn't see her through the window of the lab, so I asked to speak with her. A petite, blond hair, blue eyed, five foot two, beautiful lady came out. Both of us weren't looking for romance, but dinner after all of the time on the phone sounded and looked good. We began dating in January, 1999 and I found out Mary was a Kansas girl. She has not been further south than Amarillo, so we planned a trip to Laredo, Texas, in August. While driving there I reached up and hit the mole on top of my left ear. It began to bleed a bunch, and I told Mary, my doctor was Cryogenically freezing the mole. He already had 1 treatment done, but never said when the next should be done. I was advised by Mary that when we got back home, I was changing doctors to her's. After a good time in Laredo, and Nuevo Laredo, Mexico, we returned and Mary set me up with her doctor. Who in turn set me up with a surgeon to remove my mole. In September, 1999, my mole and I were divorced from one another. It took nine months and Mary had me on my back, in a hospital room having surgery. I woke up as the surgeon was finishing and was talking to another about having lunch. I was hungry and they mentioned PIZZA! A few days later we dropped by the lab at the hospital and saw the Doctor in the hall. He told Mary her thoughts were positive about my mole, it was MELANOMA! I asked what Melanoma was and it's described as the most aggressive skin cancer. It also can return at any time, anywhere in your body, after it has been removed and be more deadly. It has been reported to return to people ten years later and more, and be fatal then. When Melanoma enters your body, it can end up in any vital organ and spread fast. I was referred to an Oncologist in Amarillo, who said there was nothing he could do for me, but refer me to M D Anderson Cancer Center, in Houston, Texas. A highly recommended cancer center, and over six hundred eighty plus miles from Dalhart, Texas. I told Mary that I wouldn't put her through this, after all we haven't been dating long and had no idea of my future. She advised me, NOT on her watch, that was going to happen! We got the referral done for M D Anderson and purchased two airline tickets to Houston, Texas. This was in October, 1999, that is how dangerous Melanoma can be. We called M D Anderson before we went and they had a couple of motels on their list that helped cancer patient's and family's. A taxi from the airport, to the motel and a rest until our appointment the next day. The motel had bus rides all day long to the hospital, so that helped. Our first day at M D Anderson was like the first day at a new school. There are signs and maps everywhere, elevators also, plenty, many floors, corridors, rooms and so much more. At first sight, it's a very intimidating large hospital, but it is clearly marked and we were to see an Oncologist for head, ears, nose and throat. The sign showed what floor, and once on that floor it was marked where to go. My Oncologist was Doctor Gillenwater, and she was ready with our records we had brought and others that were faxed. After a general check-up, at forty four years young, I was in pretty good shape. I was given an itinerary of appointments at M D Anderson, I was to follow for the rest of the week. My Doctor G. explained to us, the surgery that removed the mole didn't have good margins. I suppose I was thinking, take the damn ear, but leave me with enough to hang my glasses on! I was also told I had a fifty fifty chance. I should have asked, does that mean a chance of living, dying, or none of the above? One of the tests I was set up to take, was called, "Lymphoscintigraphy" essentially this is Lymph Node Mapping. The Lymph Nodes in our body are like small Volkswagen bugs, They transport a blood like fluid throughout our bodies and are about the size of a pea. They also transport cancer and diseases and need to be checked near the areas affected with cancer. In my case the doctors needed to see if the

Lymph Nodes on the left side of my face, drained behind my ear, or in front of my ear. If surgery was needed the Lymph Nodes would be removed leaving a scar. That would be on my face if they drained on the front side. The test showed behind my ear and down my neck. I get to keep my great looks and not be competing with Frankenstein. After all, he was thrown together and I was …..? My next test and most embarrassing, was called Mole Mapping. You lay on a table naked, while in my case a young Female technician begins to look at your body from top to bottom, front to back and side to side. They mark on a diagram of a body, every Mole they find, size and color. I mean they look everywhere! Before the mapping began I looked at Mary and decided my modesty is gone, Mary can stay! I had the usual blood testing, x-rays and cat scans done and then I was escorted into a very small room, where a doctor began to prod around on my neck. I asked if Mary could be in there, and was advised, no! A nurse entered the room with a large syringe with a needle big enough to make a Samurai warrior proud to carry. I began to pucker up thinking, OUCH this is going to hurt! A suspicious Lymph Node was felt, and he was going in for a sample of it. I was laying there thinking of all of the stupid things I've done in my past, and now I was going to die of a very large needle in my neck. My Lymph Node juice went to a lab for testing, and we went back to rest at the motel. The next test was a general viewing of my mouth, gums and teeth to see if any issues were found, such as a bad tooth needing to be pulled or repaired. No problems were found and then a mold was made of my teeth, top and bottom, just in case Radiation was warranted. Our doctor advised us of the Lymph Node juice and the initial surgery's margins were not good. She told us that Radiation Treatments were a possibility, and in my case, Interferon would be used after I got over the surgery and all. After Mary and I talked, we called and advised that we were ready. This was Friday and it was set up for Monday, so we rented a car and went to Galveston, walked on the beach, did some shopping and enjoyed ourselves. On Monday morning I went into surgery to remove more of my ear for better margins, and the suspicious Lymph Node in my neck that came back positive with Melanoma. This was major surgery that started behind my left ear, around the back of my ear and down my neck then across to the middle of my throat. I woke up in the recovery room and Mary was with me. Not in the bed, but sitting in a chair holding my hand. I didn't jump up and say I was hungry, like the removal of the mole, but my neck was wrapped like I was in the Arctic Circle and I barely could move it. The doctor came in and advised us of how the surgery went. She said a nerve was cut while trying to get a Lymph Node out, and It may cause me problems later on, and also Forty Lymph Nodes were removed and sent to the lab for testing. We would have to wait and see the lab results, before setting up the next steps. I had to stay in jail...the hospital a couple of days, to make sure I was able to travel. When I was released and getting ready to leave, a phlebotomist came in and took my blood. Afterwards I felt like my blood pressure had gone up too high. A nurse began to take my blood pressure by pumping up the BP Cuff, and where the lab tech removed my blood, began squirting out blood. This upset the nurse, and Mary saw it grabbed a cloth and applied pressure. I had to laugh and tell the nurse it was OK, because she was so worried. Everything went well after that, we checked out of the motel, headed to the airport, and that's when we were treated well by receiving a cart ride with our luggage, to the airline gate. We then were the first to be able to take our seats, before anyone else. The flight back to Amarillo was rough for everyone aboard. The pilot must have taken a bumpy cloud run, to save time getting there. It was close to the end of October, we're home finally and Halloween was a few days away. I told Mary since my neck is full of staples, from my ear to the middle of my throat, I would sit on the front porch and give out candy. That went well and I didn't have to dress for the occasion. We finally received a call from Doctor Gillenwater about the forty Lymph Nodes removed. There were three that came back positive for Melanoma. I would need Radiation to the ear, neck and throat. After that was over I would go on a routine of Interferon. This sounded like a rough journey ahead. I called Mary at work and she came home. When she walked into the house, I did what a man should do, I lost it and started to cry. I told her of the next process I needed to begin after getting the staples out and healing from the surgery. I have always taken my own stitches out, when I could see and reach them. The staples must be easy as stitches, so I was going to remove them myself. Absolutely no one told me that the staple ends bend together after being inserted. I grabbed the first one pulled and decided to let someone who does this type of removal, a doctor! I started my Radiation treatments in Amarillo, Texas at the Don and Sybil Harrington Cancer Center, on December 02, 1999. My previous visit there was to meet Doctor John Gwadzds. Doctor Gwadzds advised me of what to expect and hopefully what it will accomplish. A mask was made to bolt and hold my head still to the table, while receiving the Radiation treatments. This is where the molds that were made at M D Anderson, of my teeth were to be used to protect my teeth. I received two heavy Radiation treatments to my neck and face, per week, for five total.

While receiving the treatments, I was watching an interesting light show that somewhat eased my fear of the Radiation. When I told Doctor Gwadzds of the light show, he said there was no light show. It was due to being so close to my eyes and head/brain and the amount used. The treatments didn't hurt at all and my last one was December sixteenth, 1999, Extensive, Precise, and Effective, I hoped! I woke up with the most horrible, sore throat I have ever had. My throat and the side of my neck were burned and it shows from the Burn Scars on my neck, from the heavy doses of Radiation. I was given pain medication and thought to myself, Self, if I can't swallow anything, they must expect me to shove these pills up my butt! The pain finally subsided and one evening while I was shaving, the hair by my left ear and up to an inch or so came out in clumps, never to return! I was given thirty days to recover, before Interferon treatments would start. Interferon is natural proteins produced by our cells of the Immune system. In January, 2000, I was evaluated prior to the beginning and it's like adding an Octane booster to your gasoline. It boosts your Immune system, to help fight off unwanted dangerous cells in your body, such as cancer cells. The treatment begins with a shunt in my hand and a bag containing Interferon and one to flush it into your system. This was hung and dripped in slowly. The shunt was changed every week and the drip was done three times a week, for one month. The Interferon upset my stomach and wasn't very good for my appetite. The first month was kind of a social get together. Patients with different cancers would be in the same room having treatments, talking about how they were doing, and the Hope from treatments with recovery. It was very emotional for some and others just listened afraid of what to say. After the IV drip was over in thirty days, I was given two options, number one, self injection of Interferon, with a needle, number two, drive to Amarillo which was about eighty five miles from Dalhart, to have the shots. There was no way I was going to stick a needle in myself, so I picked option number three, Mary! If Mary didn't mind giving me Interferon shots, about three times a week, for the next eleven months I'm in. Mary was a Medical Technologist with over twenty years experience, with needles, taking blood and testing it. She agreed to give me the shots and with her doing it I was happy, sick and sore. I was doing well on the shots, losing weight but tolerating the Interferon. It's very hard on your body and what your taste buds like. I am a chocolate lover, hamburger was big on my list also, along with most everything else. I couldn't stand to smell hamburger cooking, much less eat it. Even chocolate was an enemy. All I could eat was Chinese Egg Fu Young, and packages of Ramen noodle, chicken flavored soup. The doctors kept an eye on my blood count, as Interferon knocks your immune system to practically nothing. I thought it was supposed to strengthen it. When my White blood cells got low, it showed there was a battle going on inside of me. We had bought a home and moved to Amarillo, and I transferred from the Dalhart Prison to the Clements Prison there. Mary took another job, making it three she was working. One of them was in Clayton, New Mexico hospital, part time Medical Technologist. We stayed in a hospital funded motel that had a Continental Breakfast. It was very nice and while Mary was getting ready for work one morning, I was indulging in the breakfast, to take to our room to eat. I headed back to the room and began feeling shaky, weird, out of place. As I entered the room I began to spill some milk and slur my words. From the look on my face, Mary knew I wasn't joking around and something was wrong. I went to work with her and they did some testing and after talking to my cancer doctors in Amarillo, came up with a TIA-mini stroke. It left no side effects, except piano playing while singing and doing crossword puzzles blindfolded. Which I couldn't do before. The shots continued, with more weight loss and weakness. When Mary headed to work one morning, I decided to work in the backyard to get some exercise and help keep up my strength, plus pass some time. She got home and decided to lay down for a little rest. I layed down with her and we were talking about the day, when I began to slur my words again, but much worse than before. Our nextdoor neighbor was a nurse and Mary ran over to see if she could help. When they returned, I was coming out of it. She looked me over and advised me to call the doctor in the morning. We did just that and he said give it a couple of days and we will see. We left for Goodland, Kansas, to visit Mary's family for the weekend. While we were there, my doctor called and said we were going to stop the Interferon shots for good. It was too rough on my body and health. I told him No, I wanted to finish them and he finally said OK. We brought the shot with us, just in case this happened, so after being off a few days, Mary stuck me again! It didn't take long before I broke into a Cold Sweat and felt like Hell just crawled into my body. I began to shake, sweat, couldn't get warm and curled up in a bundle layed in bed, and waited for whatever was going to happen. It was much worse getting back on Interferon, than the treatments themselves. When I woke up the next morning, I was fine and even ran a marathon with a bunch of babies in diapers, NOT! I finished my treatments with no more strokes, a lot of weight loss, strength and minor issues, such as some memory loss, my right eye was my strong eye and now won't focus. I can see but it's a blur. When my wife uses the microwave, I pee my pants and forget who I am. I tried to work while going through my treatments, and was too weak. I asked for half a day and that wasn't possible. The prison part time was a ten hour day, on the weekend. This made me mad and when my time ran out I quit! One day while I was standing in our driveway, in Amarillo, a turtle came walking across it. With the heat and no stock tanks, rivers or lakes nearby, I picked him up. It turned out to be a young Snapping Turtle and in this heat he must have needed water, so that's what I did and named him, Floyd! I wanted Mary to be close to her relatives, so I looked around Kansas City, Missouri for a correctional officers job and a Sheriff's Department in Clinton, Missouri was needing one. I was hired and we were Missouri bound.

## Sheriff's Department, Henry County, Missouri

I took a job at the Sheriff's Department in Clinton, Missouri, as a jailer, night shift by myself except the Inmates and incoming prisoners. I booked in, finger printed, and took a photo of the prisoner, searched, issued them jail garb to wear and placed them in a cell. All aspects of a jailer, I was doing in a jail built many years past its prime. It was very interesting and one night a drunk was brought in, I booked him and placed him in a cell in the basement. Later on I went to check on him and when I opened the door, I was confronted by a mad drunk. He lunged at me and I stopped him, locked the door and went about my duties. The next day I think every muscle in my body hurts. All I did was stop his advance and he laid back down. On my nights off, I rode with some of the deputies and not much out of the ordinary came up. My first three month cancer checkup came, and the Ferrell

Duncan Clinic in Springfield, Missouri, was the place set up to give me my first PET SCAN, along with the usual cancer look over. The Pet Scan is done with a dose of Radioactive drug (tracer) put in your vein through an IV, and you sit back allowing it to run through your body. After a certain time, you enter a machine somewhat like a Cat Scan. The results are then sent to a trained doctor, and when the results return, the patient is advised. We received a call for a follow up visit. We arrived and the doctor told us, I have good news and bad news. The good news, NO CANCER DETECTED! Great news but what's next, do we owe an arm and a leg? The PET SCAN found an Aortic Aneurysm, on my heart, the size of, five.three centimeters. I had no idea when it happened, but it never was found in all of my testing, I can guess prior to leaving M D Anderson, when my blood pressure skyrocketed, creating the Aneurysm. Damn, I beat Melanoma for three months, and an Aneurysm on my heart is going to burst and kill me. There was that "DALTON GANG" luck showing. As life continued, we were going broke and with Mary not working due to sickness, and with the pay a jailer made, we decided to return to Texas. I took a job at the TDCJ State Jail in Austin, Texas, when 911 occurred. I couldn't find a home we could afford, and I needed my birth certificate, for the TDCJ state jail paperwork, which was packed in a box in Clinton, Missouri with Mary working on the packing and preparing our home to sell. I worked about three days in Austin, and told them of my plans to go home and begin this move over. They understood and it was due to 911, it all happened, which saved us a bunch of money looking and finding a home we could afford. With all done in Clinton, Missouri,

## Move to Palestine, Texas and TDCJ

I picked a better location to work for, Texas Department of Criminal Justice, prison, Palestine, Texas. The prisons were a short drive from Palestine, to Tennessee Colony, where five prisons are. I let the people in the offices located in Huntsville, Texas, decide which prison I should work in. They said the Beto Unit. A Maximum Security Prison, and I would be working in the Segregation Section. These inmates are locked up twenty three hours a day, one hour for recreation, locked in a cage. They were escorted, handcuffed, everywhere they went, by two Correctional Officers. When I started at Beto, I asked for B.O.Q. Bachelor Officers Quarters to stay, until our home in Missouri sold and we could move into a home in Palestine. After about a month at the BOQ, I was tired of sharing a bathroom with another room, a sloppy outdoor area around the BOQ, with beer cans filling the trash cans. The trustee inmates cleaned up the area, and inside the BOQ halls. This wasn't a place to have beer being consumed, but they did it. I went to Palestine, looked around and found an 1832 Sq. Ft. Arts and Craft home in the Historic District. I paid $32,000 for it and moved right in. I slept on the floor, and didn't have to share anything, or smell beer that had been sitting in the sun. Mary was ready to move, and was finally feeling better from having her Thyroid killed off by a Radiation Injection, and correct dosage to get her system back on track. Our home was sold in Missouri and I drove up and pulled a trailer home with just enough belongings until our furniture arrived by movers. We stayed in the home I bought, and found a larger, better home. When our furniture came, it went to the new home. We finally were settled in! The prison had the usual fights, mattress burning, drugs brought in, money also, and Correctional Officers having affairs with inmates, flowing through the system. I got along with the inmates, and treated them like people. When they did something abusive in front of a female officer, I went above and beyond my moral obligation. They and all in their bunk, got wet! The Seg unit was the inmates in gangs and had death warrants on them, tried to conduct one, or were just too mean to be in the regular population. They were allowed a three minute shower, and escorted there handcuffed, nearly every day depending on the circumstances at the time. I enjoyed my job, and on one wing we had inmates from the prison hospital, recovering from surgery. Some was from cancer, and other issues that doctors had found and removed or repaired. I talked to quite a few that were scared of dying, hurt from the surgery, or had no idea what their future looked like. I just hope that maybe I soothed their soul, and changed their ways from bad to the Gospel. I explained my cancer and treatments and how with GOD'S MERCY, I was still walking with the living. I was having PET SCANS, every six months, for five years and then once a year for another five years. After all of this was done, I took a job at the coast, as a Lighthouse! I had to go to Tyler, Texas for the scan's, and afterwards it was time to eat something. This one particular day I picked Golden Corral. I got my food and was eating when an elderly man, dressed like a Countryfied gentleman, asked if he could sit with me. I obliged him and we began talking. I told him why I was in Tyler, and after our conversation was over, he stood up, asked me if I wanted to know if my cancer would ever return? I asked how that was going to happen, while I was really thinking, another loose nut in Tyler, picked me. He reached into his pocket and pulled a long chain out that had a clear stone hanging from it, then explained; If the stone moves Clockwise, my cancer will return. If it moves Counter Clockwise, I'm free for life from cancer. I watched his hand movement, as he held the stone in front of me and he didn't move a finger. The stone moved Counter Clockwise and his remark was, you will have, no more cancer! I thanked him for the show, and said I hoped to see him again. I watched as he and his wife left Golden Corral, walked over to an old beaten up car/camper like vehicle and drove off. I should have gotten his name, because he lifted my spirits just talking to me. The show was also interesting to watch. These folks looked like they didn't have a dime to their name. When the PET SCAN results came in, I was clear. Humm, I wonder who he really was??? One morning I was getting ready for work and my heart began beating real fast. I ended up in Palestine Regional Hospital, ICU wing and was given injections to slow down my heart rate. The problem was the shot was in the stomach and it burned. My heart was going into Atrial Fibrillation, an irregular heartbeat and had nothing to do with the Aneurysm. The second time it happened, I was at work and the infirmary wouldn't allow me to leave on my own. They thought I was having a Heart Attack and called an ambulance. My truck stayed at the prison, while I was transported back to the hospital and another drug had to be used for my heart issue. I think good luck ran in my family, right out the door and never to be seen leaving. I was having bad cramps that would double me over. I found out spicy and fatty foods were an issue with my stomach. After testing my Gallbladder, it wasn't working like it should be, so it was removed. The doctor who removed it couldn't find a tag stating, Made in China, so warranty was void. Mary and I bought a couple of rental houses and rented them out. I took care of repairs and remodels were done by us both. There were two CO's and their family lived in one. I worked with his wife in Seg and he worked in General Population. He was a worker and became a good friend. One day he showed me a letter he found, from an inmate to his wife. She was having an affair under both of our noses, with a Black inmate, Cop Killer. She was escorted off the unit, they divorced and he transferred back to a prison in Amarillo, Texas. I lost a good friend! This is an all too common problem in the system, along with an arm's length of other issues, most dangerous. I began having trouble climbing the three flights of stairs, on the wings where the inmates' cells were located, and with issues pertaining to a certain Sargent and Lieutenant (drunk's and Corrupt) I decided to retire from the prison. In the time I worked there, I found one inmate who tried to hang himself, another that must have overdosed on drugs and did kill himself, seen several female officers having affairs with inmates and also bringing in contraband, one of the officers I worked with at Beto, went home and killed himself, reasons unknown, the warden was having an affair with his secretary, a girl in the office was having an affair with a married, with children, Sargent and got pregnant, and I could go on. The Palestine hospital knew me by name, because I was there visiting Mary in the lab, or laying on my back in the emergency room. We lived a few miles South of the hospital, in the country and was remodeling our home. One day

Mary was sick, laying on the couch resting. I was using a grinder on the kitchen floor, with sandpaper on the grinder and taking the glue off of the concrete. My left arm is weak and the grinder hit the wall trim by the floor, jumped back, ran up my thumb and across my wrist. I decorated the floor, refrigerator, walls, everything while I was headed to the sink. I called out to Mary, I thought she might want to look at this. After wrapping a towel around my hand and she got dressed, we visited Palestine ER. I received eighteen stitches, to add to my luck. My balance has been an issue, since the surgery and Radiation. The Nerve that was cut in my neck, was a Root Nerve, a doctor told us. I can't lift my left arm above my waist and from the left side of my face, down into my arm and shoulder, I'm numb. When I'm falling, I can't use my left arm to help catch myself. Unfortunately, it's a game, I walk, fall down, get up and do it over again, life goes on! I finally had my heart Aneurysm checked. After ten years and Melanoma hasn't killed me, maybe I should. My aneurysm has grown from a five.three Centimeter, up to a five.five Centimeter. The time came to have it repaired and I was offered three choices of valves. The first was a pig's valve, second was a cow's and the third was a Mechanical Valve. The first two would eventually have to be replaced in the future and the Mechanical Valve should out tick me. They take a licking and keep on ticking! I opted for Mechanical and surgery was set up for July 2011. I literally can hear my heart TICK, because of the surgery and Radiation on my left ear. It can keep me awake at night and I'm not complaining, but shouldn't I be dead? After Melanoma, TIA Strokes, Heart Surgery, including all of the emergency room visits and so much more? While working around the house one day, Mary received a call from my buddy, who moved back to Amarillo. I'll call him Bob and he married a lady he worked with at the prison there. They put a transfer in and bought a home in Palestine. This was a surprise to me and I couldn't wait to see them. There was a large stock tank behind our home, and I had permission to fish there. It also gave our property ambiance and value. When Bob had a day off, we would fish in the tank in a two man Bass Buster boat. After a day of fishing and not catching anything, we decided to call it quits. When we pulled up to the bank, Bob jumped out to pull the boat further up. He said hold on as I was standing and when Bob pulled, the seat came up. I went over the rear of the boat into the edge of the tank, in about a foot of murky water face first. The only part of me still in the boat were my feet, stuck on the edge and dry. I stood up covered in mud, moss and obviously soaking wet, looked at Bob who was in shock and I began to laugh. That got Bob laughing and it was something we both needed. After walking into the house and explaining to Mary what happened, she also needed a good laugh. While talking with Bob about his return to the Palestine area, he said GOD wanted him to return to help me. I learned about GOD from Bob and he was the only person I have ever met that didn't use profanity, or even had an enemy. He lost a leg when he played Football in school, after a freak accident and grew up with a prosthetic since then. Even in the prison working with Bob, I couldn't keep up with him. If an inmate gave him trouble, Bob would yank off his leg and threaten the inmate with it. We would laugh, even the inmate and all was forgotten. One day Bob quit the prison and started to deliver travel trailers with a one ton truck, from up North, to California. His brother James, got him into the delivery service and they were both delivering trailers. I received a call one day that Bob was in a hospital in Tyler, Texas. While on the road delivering and heading back to get another, a major headache came to Bob, and he had a relative help get him home to the doctor. They found a tumor in his brain that turned out to be a Glioblastoma. It was a very aggressive tumor and was removed. After his recovery, Bob went back to delivering. One day his brothers came to our home and we were shooting guns, when I noticed Bob looked like he was having a problem. He said he was OK and I had no reason to doubt him. I received a call that Bob was back in the hospital and the Glioblastoma had grown back. My friend, fishing buddy was dying and nothing could be done except ease the pain and be with him. The family was called to see Bob, while he was conscious and able to talk. I stopped by the hospital often, and spent the night there with him, so his wife and family could go home, clean up and rest. I was talking with Bob and he knew he was dying and wasn't scared of it happening. He was a religious man, who was close to GOD and the BIBLE. They transferred Bob home, so he could be close to his family when it occurred and not in a hospital. His body was already in a Coma and I took off to pick up a package out of town. That evening I received the call, Bob had passed away. He returned to Palestine to help me, and it turned out I was to be with him while he was dying. I lost a very good friend and fishing buddy on March First, 2013, almost two years after Bob was at the hospital after my heart surgery. I was at the funeral with the family, saying goodbye to an old friend.

Picture of obit to go here

## Moving to Deep East Texas Forest Life

We purchased a piece of property out of Lufkin, Texas, in the Piney Forest of Deep East Texas. It was a remodel on two acres with acres around us to hunt or explore in. We worked on the home, while Mary lived in a travel trailer on the property and worked at the hospital. I drove back and forth working on both properties, the one for sale, and the one we purchased. When Mary started her job in Lufkin, I needed time to fix the furnace and water coming into the home. It was too cold to live in the home, but not too cold to watch her Kansas City Chiefs on our large TV which was too big for the travel trailer. We took the next three years remodeling this home, while issues at the hospital management deteriorated. We took a ride to San Angelo, Texas, after Mary had a talk with management about a job. She was hired by Shannon Healthcare, rented a one room efficiency apartment, until our home sold. I stayed and finished up some work, put a new floor in a sixteen foot trailer that would move a bunch of our stuff, and a trailer hitch on the rear of it for our smoker to be pulled. Before Mary left to go to work there I was moving the back deck I had built, to where it was supposed to go, with my tractor. I couldn't get it to release from the tractor and got my largest crowbar to get it loose. When I put pressure on the deck, the crowbar slipped and hit me in the left temple. I ended up with a black eye, and headaches. I have to take a pill to relieve them and I tried to quit but my headache comes back. On December 27, 2016, Mary came back to Lufkin and helped me pack. She picked out a house in San Angelo and it was ready for us to move in. When our movers finished loading and left, Mary did the same thing and was to meet them there. This was at the end of December. We would be in our new home one day in 2016, as soon as I got there. I loaded up our cats in the cat carriers, a chicken in a cage (pet) and the two dogs with me in the truck. We pulled in that evening late, truck, trailer, smoker on wheels, all animals home at last. I found a doctor as soon as I could and updated him with my medical records. I lost my voice after the surgery on my heart. My ear, nose and throat doctor in Palestine, looked down my throat and couldn't see any issues. It was hard to understand me and was getting worse. Even the doctors in Lufkin had no idea, so we figured it was from the cancer surgery and Radiation. My doctor at Shannon, in San Angelo, referred me to an Ear, Nose, Throat, here and after looking at my vocal cords, one set was Paralyzed. He wasn't sure if it was from cancer surgery and Radiation, or when they Intubated me before doing my heart surgery. So we decided, all of the above and the doctor said he could give me a shot in my Paralyzed vocal cord and see if that helped. It was done as an Outpatient at the hospital, and I had to be put under, due to it hurting. After it was done, and healed, my voice was back. I loved it, but it didn't last too long, so he did it again, the same way with the same results. I have a bad time talking and folks understand me. Most of the time on the phone, I hear the words, YES MA'AM!

It's hard to tell them I'm a guy, so I just keep talking. My insurance man/friend has an issue with his voice, and put us together you would think we were a comedy act. Put Mary with me and you'd have a human jigsaw. I can't speak and be understood and she can't hear. It's like watching a scene from the Beverly Hillbillies on TV, Grandma meets Grandpa from the Real McCoys. We can live with it and life goes on, sort of. I have swallowing issues to go with all of my throat and vocal cords. When I swallow something, solid food or water, my pipeline has trouble. If it's food and even chewed up, it gets stuck in my throat and I choke on it. When this happens, a drink of water sometimes helps. Other times It backs up from my stomach and I aspirate. The valve in my throat separating where food or air goes, is damaged, thus aspiration is occurring. If I swallow too big of a drink of water or fluid, it takes the wrong path and I choke leading to some aspiration. It's a crap shoot when I eat, or drink. When Covid came into the picture, our country went into a Panic Mode. My wife, Mary retired just before it hit and the hospital was full of Covid patients. When we saw the masks being worn and the useless amount of help they accomplished, we decided to NOT wear them. Then after finding out what was in the Covid shot, and the effects associated with the shot, Mary, a forty plus year Medical Technologist, decided we would pass on the Covid shots. I was fine with her decision and after going to bed one night, I was having trouble catching my breath. I layed there hoping it was a short issue and would go away. It was getting worse so I woke Mary up, and by then I needed help fast. She called an ambulance and they were here quickly, and we headed to the hospital. A bunch of tests were started, and the hospital staff thought it was Covid. It turned out to be Pneumonia and the Covid test was negative! I spent three days in the hospital, taking a strong drug to cure me and the fluid on my lungs. After being released from the hospital, I had a follow-up appointment with my doctor, about a week later. That evening I was getting sick and had a clinic test for Covid. I caught it and maybe from the hospital. This time I stayed home and about three days later I was doing fine. A few weeks went by with nothing happening to me, and then my luck ran out. I couldn't breathe and this time was worse than the first. I was headed downhill fast. Another ambulance ride and stay in the hospital with Pneumonia, and this was a worse case than the last. Since I already had Covid, they put me on the Covid wing until a room somewhere else in the hospital came available. I spent two days on the Covid wing and one on a regular wing. While getting IV bags of a strong antibiotic that worked. Again, everything was going well and I was released to go home. I always slept with my bedroom window open, regardless of the temperature. I even built my bed frame high enough so the mattress was the height of the windowsill. This gave me a small problem crawling into bed without some help from a step up. My step up was an old kitchen chair that I have been using to crawl into bed for years, but this night proved to be my last. I stepped up on the chair and must have done some Break Dancing. I fell, hitting the chest of drawers and landing somewhat on the floor and the chair. The floor broke my fall, left shoulder and wrist. I could see my wrist was broken, due to the direction it was pointing and hurt. I called Mary into the bedroom, and asked her to move the chair, but let me get myself up. We headed to the hospital, where x-rays were done and I was advised of surgery to my wrist adding a metal brace to hold it together. The surgery was done the next morning and after a day or so in the hospital, I was released. I was in pain, still out of it,

and became a hazard for Mary at home without help. She called
the hospital back, and a doctor advised Mary to bring me back. I
spent a total of two weeks in the hospital, and then had to go for
rehabilitation. When this first began, the doctors decided to allow
my shoulder to heal by itself, because of the surgery being major,
if they had to go in and repair it. It healed but is out of place a bit.
A large bone pushes up on top of my shoulder, but gives me no
pain. I'm numb in my left arm, from the Melanoma surgery and the
Nerve that was cut . I finally got back to my regular life, cutting the
grass, weed-eating the areas needed, everything was good. I
work with wood building things, and also make cages for small
wild animals. Mary and I rehabilitate the young that are found
without their mother and return to the wild when they are big
enough. This started with Opossums, Racoons, a Porcupine,
Skunk, and a few bird's. Then someone called about a baby
Squirrel, eyes not open yet and we said yes. That followed with
two more Squirrels from different areas, two young Racoons and
two Opossums. The young Racoons grew fast and were the first
to be released. Then an Opossum was released. I was doing
good until I hit myself in the stomach climbing up on a trash bin to
retrieve two old Wood Pocket Doors. My stomach acid came up,
and I tried hard to get rid of it without breathing it in. I knew what
was coming, so I went into the house, told Mary of Aspirating and
how It happened. She began to monitor my oxygen intake and
ability to breath. It didn't take long, and I was in trouble. We
rushed to the hospital, and were immediately placed on oxygen,
blood was taken, and a stent was placed in my arm. An x-ray was
done of my lungs, then Mary was told it didn't look good, be
prepared. I had a note on my medical reports, that I didn't want to
be placed on the Ventilator, and a, do not resuscitate. I remember

a doctor telling me if I don't go on the vent, I will go home to die. He told me I would have a Bronchoscopy done, while on the vent, and remove as much of mucus and foreign material out of my lungs as possible. Mary and I agreed it would be better to have this, than the inevitable result if I went home. I remember Mary being allowed in the room where I was and she would ask me if I wanted her to read from the BIBLE. I agreed and she read the Gospel. This went on everytime she was there and I had no idea how long she was there or stayed. I was put to sleep long enough to hook up the machine, and stayed in La La Land until it was finished with its job. I don't remember much of the treatments, or time and whatever they gave me to become incoherent, helped my imagination go wild. I came up with so many crazy thoughts, I must have given the nurses and staff a good laugh. I thought I was in a special hospital for major vehicle accident victims, major health issues such as mine, and was there for the helicopter drop offs with the best of the best Trauma Doctors available. The hospital was on a military base, shaped like a saucer with five floors. The first two were above ground and the bottom floor was the chow hall. When I was moved out of ICU, I was placed in an area needing complete remodel. It was an older section by the looks of it. Remember, while I was on the ventilator, I was kept on a drug to keep me calm. I wasn't fed by regular food and the only water I could have was ice chunks. I was hungry, thirsty and ready to leave. I entered on September 24th, 2022, it must have been three or four days and I wanted to go home! My wife Mary said I was on the vent for eight days, and in the hospital about three weeks. I was so weak, I couldn't wipe my own butt. Heck, I wasn't even sure where it was anymore! I was finally allowed to go to a rehabilitation physicality, and they would help me

strengthen my body. This was the only place I've been in that had such good food, that close neighborhood folks came to buy, to go meals. I spent five days there and after begging to go home due to Mary taking all of the burden and I missed our two dogs, four cats, three squirrels, and three opossums, Mary was taking care of. On my first follow up visit to my doctor, I asked Mary to show me where I was at in the hospital. I was looking for the saucer shaped building and she pointed to the hospital, as we drove by. I had her drive me around it, I was so sure of what I remembered I needed to prove it to her. We never had a honeymoon when we married, because I was on my treatments for Melanoma. After those were finished, Mary had trouble with her Thyroid and opted for a Radioactive iodine over surgery, to kill it off. Then getting her system back on track by medication took a while and with us moving to Clinton, Missouri, Mary had to find another doctor to help her. In the years since then, Mary has been diagnosed with several Auto-Immune diseases, and has messed up her whole system. We don't eat out any more, hardly go anywhere, I miss fishing, and we now enjoy ourselves at home. My voice is bad and hard to understand, but it doesn't matter, Mary can't hear me anyway. This is a totally different way of life, than what I was used to before I was diagnosed with Melanoma, but it's a life I'm proud to help others with, Enrichment, Courage, Love, Hope and most importantly, FAITH! Mary has stayed with me through thick and thin, while having issues herself. She is my Angel sent from GOD! There are many places to acquire information on every type of cancer that exists. Here are just a few names and addresses. I promise they will inform as well as prepare you for what may be.
#1 The American Cancer Society Cancer Response System
    1-800 ACS-2345, or www.cancer.org

#2 The National Cancer Institute Cancer Information Service
 (CIS) 1-800-422-6237 or www.cancernet.nci.nih.gov

#3 Melanoma Research Foundation
   1-800-mrf-1290 or www.melanoma.org

#4 The American Academy of Dermatology
   708-330-0230 or www.aad.org

 The best place to buy UPF clothing, I have purchased caps, hats, shirts from, is Coolibar,

Made in the USA
Coppell, TX
23 June 2025